CONTEN

Poetry Book Society

CHOICE RECOMMENDATION SPECIAL COMMENDATION SELECTORS	SANDEEP PARMAR & VIDYAN RAVINTHIRAN
TRANSLATION SELECTOR	GEORGE SZIRTES
PAMPHLET SELECTORS	A.B. JACKSON & DEGNA STONE
WILD CARD SELECTOR	ANTHONY ANAXAGOROU
CONTRIBUTORS	SOPHIE O'NEILL NATHANIEL SPAIN
EDITORIAL & DESIGN	ALICE KATE MULLEN

Membership Options

Associate 4 *Bulletins* a year (UK £22, Europe £35, Rest of the World £42)
Full 4 Choice books and 4 *Bulletins* a year (£55, £65, £75)
Charter 20 books and 4 *Bulletins* (£180, £210, £235)
Education 4 books, 4 *Bulletins*, posters, teaching notes (£79, £89, £99)
Charter Education 20 books, 4 *Bulletins*, posters, teaching notes (£209, £245, £275)
Translation 4 Translation books and 4 *Bulletins* (£65, £90, £99)
Student 4 Choice books and 4 *Bulletins* (£35, £55, £65)
Translation Plus Full 4 Choices, 4 *Bulletins* & 4 Translation books (£98, £120, £132)
Translation Plus Charter 20 books, 4 *Bulletins* & 4 Translation books (£223, £265, £292)
Single copies £6
Cover Art "Untitled", from the series *The Accidental Theorist*, 2007
© Edgar Martins (www.edgarmartins.com)

ISBN 9781999858971 ISSN 0551-1690

Supported using public funding by
ARTS COUNCIL ENGLAND

Poetry Book Society | Churchill House | 12 Mosley Street |
Newcastle upon Tyne | NE1 1DE | 0191 230 8100 | pbs@inpressbooks.co.uk

WWW.POETRYBOOKS.CO.UK

LETTER FROM THE PBS

We hope you like our bold new-look cover for this Winter *Bulletin*. The New Horizons cover series is now complete and we have moved on to explore contemporary photography starting with the internationally renowned Edgar Martins. If you would like to buy any missed *Bulletins* to complete your collection, or give them as a gift-set this Christmas, please do get in touch.

We are delighted to announce Raymond Antrobus as this season's selected Choice poet. He writes, "This is a book the child I was needed to see, and the adult I am needed to write". We feel it is the book everyone needs to read.

We're proud to see the selections this season coming from a mix of publishing houses, including a broad range of independent publishers from across the UK. This reflects our mission to encourage all publishers regardless of size or location to submit their poets' work, enabling our selectors to pick from the broadest possible range of contemporary poetry.

The PBS and Mslexia competition winners will be announced just after this *Bulletin* goes to press – please keep your eyes on our newsletter and website for news of the winning poets later this month.

For those of you who live in, or would like an excuse to visit London, please do join us for our most ambitious event yet. No One is an Island takes place on Friday 23rd November at St Martin Within Ludgate church. Raymond Antrobus and David Harsent will perform their work and a fusion of metaphysical poetry spanning the 17th to 21st century, accompanied by live music. It will be a complete treat.

Talking of treats, please remember you can give the gift of poetry this Christmas! We have many gift membership options and would be so happy to help you spread your love of poetry further afield. All gift members receive a welcome pack containing a free poetry book and a £10 book voucher. Details can be found online, or please do call us for more information.

We've also included a little gift for you from the PBS and One Plum Poem in your winter parcel. This specially commissioned card features a new poem by Carol Ann Duffy to mark her last Christmas as Poet Laureate. The full range of One Plum Poem cards is now available on our website. We do hope you enjoy them!

SOPHIE O'NEILL, PBS & INPRESS DIRECTOR

RAYMOND ANTROBUS

Raymond Antrobus was born in London, Hackney, to an English mother and Jamaican father and is the author of *To Sweeten Bitter* and *The Perseverance*. He is a founding member of Chill Pill and Keats House Poets Forum and the recipient of fellowships from Cave Canem, Complete Works 3 and Jerwood Compton Poetry. He is also one of the world's first recipients of an MA in Spoken Word education from Goldsmiths University. In 2018 he was awarded The Geoffrey Dearmer Prize.

THE PERSEVERANCE

PENNED IN THE MARGINS | £9.99 | PBS PRICE £7.50

POETRY BOOK SOCIETY CHOICE

RAYMOND
THE ANTROBUS
PERSEVERANCE

'Raymond Antrobus is as searching a poet as you're
likely to find writing today' —KAVEH AKBAR

Penned in *the Margins*

Several currents run through Raymond Antrobus' phenomenal debut, *The Perseverance*, and each, like a wave bound to its element, conjoins and diverges with the force of its nature. Locked occasionally to form (the sestina, a "broken ghazal") or influence, Antrobus' poems sift questions of identity, deafness, language, sound and mutability through several narratives including the death of a father. Mythically proportioned in retrospect, the father is a counterpoint here for the grown son to evaluate his own making and being in the world. The collection's titular poem phrases unforgettably the perseverance of complex filial love: "We lose our fathers before we know it." But what is perhaps most exceptional about this book is its writing back to educational bias, ableism, violence against the other. In 'Dear Hearing World', Antrobus takes his cue from Danez Smith's anti-racist work and applies it to the destructive limits applied to deafness, where the partial rhyme of "spine" and "assigned" hints at subsequent, broader systemic power.

> You erased what could have always been poetry.
> You taught me I was inferior to standard English expression —
> I was a broken speaker, you were never a broken interpreter —
> taught me my speech was dry for someone who should sound
> like they're underwater. It took years to talk with a straight spine
> and mute red marks on the coursework you assigned.

Among these rejoinders is the remarkable crossing out of Ted Hughes' 1980s poem 'Deaf School'. Hughes' poem can only be read now as offensive; it reflects a system based on a presupposition that deaf children are intellectually "simple". Elsewhere, Antrobus rightly takes aim at the origins of this damaging thinking, which he finds in the life and work of Alexander Bell (and, intriguingly, via Bell's deaf wife and mother) and other historical depictions of "disability".

Ultimately, this book is a brave and necessary rethinking of the ways in which we perceive and, indeed, the language through which we persevere.

SANDEEP PARMAR

RAYMOND ANTROBUS

"I use perseverance in this mad city" – Kendrick Lamar

The Perseverance is a collection of poems that ranges across histories and continents. It's a book of loss, contested language (including sign language) and praise. Throughout the book elegies for my father find a place alongside meditations on deafness. I also interviewed some Deaf friends of mine who work in education and the arts about their stories for the book. What struck me doing this, was that every one of them was surprised why anyone would find their lives interesting, but I hope now they feature in a book they'll see something new and valuable in their stories.

Looking back at writing *The Perseverance* now I notice how many shapes of the poems are podiums or pillars, blocks of speech trying to hold each word and idea up on the page. A lot of the book is deliberately conversational. How I hear isn't always what is actually said but in poetry it can still have a place that transcends the sound etiquettes of the hearing world: "...Tabitha's aunt is all mumble. She either said do you want a pancake? or you look melancholic..."

The Perseverance also challenges how deaf people are seen as "people without language". A Ted Hughes poem gets re-evaluated, as does a Charles Dickens short story. A lot of the poems are attempts to assert deafness as a way of being, that are multi-dimensional, poems that cannot be dismissed as pure "identity politics". In some ways *The Perseverance* is an ode to language, communication and the NHS. It's a book the child I was needed to see, and the adult I am needed to write. *The Perseverance*, I hope, is understood as more than a poetry collection, it is a document, an elegiac talking history book.

RAYMOND RECOMMENDS

The Republic Of Motherhood by Liz Berry (Chatto); *Blues for Mister Charlie*, a play by James Baldwin; *Us* by Zaffar Kunial (Faber); *Millennial Roost* by Dustin Pearson (Eyewear Publishing); *Life In A Box Is A Pretty Life* by Dawn Lundy Martin (Nightboat Books); *Citizen Illegal* by José Olivarez (BreakBeat Poets).

I CHOICE

DEAR HEARING WORLD

after Danez Smith

I have left Earth in search of sounder orbits,
a solar system where the space between
a star and a planet isn't empty. I have left
a white beard of noise in my place and many
of you won't know the difference. We are
indeed the same volume, all of us eventually fade.
I have left Earth in search of an audible God.
I do not trust the sound of yours.
You wouldn't recognise my grandmother's *Hallelujah*
if she had to sign it, you would have made her sit
on her hands and put a ruler in her mouth
as if measuring her distance from holy.
Take your God back, though his songs
are beautiful, they are not loud enough.

I want the fate of Lazarus for every deaf school
you've closed, every deaf child whose confidence
has gone to a silent grave, every BSL user
who has seen the annihilation of their language,
I want these ghosts to haunt your tongue-tied hands.
I have left Earth, I am equal parts sick of your
oh, I'm hard of hearing too, just because
you've been on an airplane or suffered head colds.
Your voice has always been the loudest sound in a room.

I call you out for refusing to acknowledge
sign language in classrooms, for assessing
deaf students on what they can't say
instead of what they can, we did not ask to be a part
of the hearing world, I can't hear my joints crack
but I can feel them. I am sick of sounding out your rules —
you tell me I breathe too loud and it's rude to make noise
when I eat, sent me to speech therapists, said I was speaking
a language of holes, I was pronouncing what I heard
but your judgment made my syllables disappear,
your magic master trick hearing world — drowning out the quiet,
bursting all speech bubbles in my graphic childhood,
you are glad to benefit from audio supremacy,
I tried, hearing people, I tried to love you, but you laughed
at my deaf grammar, I used commas not full stops
because everything I said kept running away,
I mulled over long paragraphs because I didn't know
what a *natural break* sounded like, ~~you erased~~
~~what could have always been poetry~~

You erased what could have always been poetry.
You taught me I was inferior to standard English expression
I was a broken speaker, you were never a broken interpreter —
taught me my speech was dry for someone who should sound
like they're underwater. It took years to talk with a straight spine
and mute red marks on the coursework you assigned.

Deaf voices go missing like sound in space
and I have left earth to find them.

CARRIE ETTER

Carrie Etter grew up in Normal, Illinois, lived for thirteen years in southern California and has resided in England since 2001. She has published three previous collections, most recently *Imagined Sons* (Seren, 2014), shortlisted for the Ted Hughes Award for New Work in Poetry, and edited two other works, including *Infinite Difference: Other Poetries by UK Women Poets* (Shearsman, 2010). She is Reader in Creative Writing at Bath Spa University and lives in Bath with her husband, the potter Trevor Lillistone and two cats, Max and Susu. You can find her at carrietter.com and @Carrie_Etter.

THE WEATHER IN NORMAL

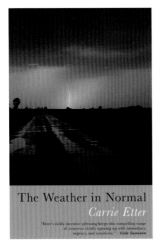

The Weather in Normal
Carrie Etter

"Etter's richly inventive phrasing keeps this compelling range of concerns vividly opening up with immediacy, urgency, and sensitivity." *Cole Swensen*

SEREN | £9.99 | PBS PRICE £7.50

Sometimes, reading a poem, we're pulled up short by one word in particular. It seems to have wandered in from elsewhere, to not really belong – until you look more closely. In 'My Father and the Blizzard' Carrie Etter writes touchingly of a parent's death: "his wife sat bedside   as a nurse bestowed morphine //   all windows gone white". Honours, blessings upon a marriage – these things are bestowed: to have that formal word arrive in this context catches us off guard. It ritualises the act, seeming to prolong and cherish an instance of medical care (contrasted with the brisk, brusque phrases which bookend it). The same fine attention to a single word appears in 'Eldest', where, seeing her father in his hospital room, the speaker tells herself: "Now you must gentle". A verb, not an adjective. She must calm him and herself. Animals, too, can be "gentled": this is poetry about the farming community of Normal, Illinois – weather-embattled and economically unsure – where that word "normal", on the book's cover, can be read two ways. Once our parents die, we must accept a new normal: Etter's are poems of grief, but also of (new) beginnings, of false starts and true starts. Remembering her father on the CB radio – during another blizzard – she homes in once more on a single word:

> I – nine? ten? – stand in the dining room's peripheral darkness
> and watch him flick dials,
> switch between the emergency channel
> and our usual and back again.
> My father grows smaller –
> can one *grow* – yes, he grows – smaller,
> he sweats, he calls again, he begs,
> he says *she was going to Zayre's*, he says

"Growing" is very much of the essence. Etter writes of the stoicism of farmers confronted with drought-killed crops: "It's a wonder," says one, "we aren't all alcoholics." She also writes vividly and angrily about climate change, about disappearing butterflies for instance; her poems, experimentally arranged and disarranged, suggest – amid white space her text-fragments show like snow-surrounded cinders – the afterlife of what has been lost. Lingering echoes, of parents, vanished ecosystems: "consider the absences".

SELECTOR'S COMMENT   VIDYAN RAVINTHIRAN

CARRIE ETTER

I remember first talking to a few friends about a book to be called *The Weather in Normal* only a couple of years after I moved to England in 2001. Perhaps the distance from home gave rise to the idea, while the events of the years between conception (say, 2003) and composition (2013-17) resulted in a very different book from the one I originally imagined.

The weather and the landscape always figured in the work, but my parents' horrible deaths in 2009 and 2011 resulted in a book that is as much an elegy for my Illinois, the place and the people, as it is an ode to it. It is a book of three acts or arcs: the death of my parents, the sale of our family home and the effects of climate change on the state. The sense of place, in its weather, flora, and fauna, permeates the whole.

One of the great adventures in reading or writing a book of poetry lies in the nature of its engagement with form and in composing *The Weather in Normal,* I experienced something I think of as a formal restlessness: there are free-verse couplets, a long open field poem, prose poems, even a long poem that draws on English alliterative verse in its use of a central caesura. An endorsement for my first pamphlet in 1998 spoke of it as "quite a ride," and that seems apt for this work, too, at least for my experience in writing it.

As *The Weather in Normal* was coming to fruition, I was pleased to see it begin and end with odes. It seems important, amid the mourning for parents and the anger and grief over climate change, that we cherish and that this be a book that also cherishes.

CARRIE RECOMMENDS

I've recently read and heartily recommend Anne Carson's *Float* and *Nox* (Cape and New Directions), Evie Shockley's *semiautomatic* (Wesleyan), Terrance Hayes' *American Sonnets for My Past and Future Assassin* (Penguin) and Rosmarie Waldrop's *White Is A Color* (Guillemot). In other genres, I've also admired Deborah Levy's *The Cost of Living* (Hamish Hamilton) and Shaun Tan's *Tales from Outer Suburbia* (McClelland and Stewart). Indeed, I've loved all these books so much I want to read everything these authors have written.

RECOMMENDATION

The weather belongs to everyone

Image: 'Thunderstorm Lightning – Central Illinois' by Jason P. Ross

SCAR

i.m. Peter Reading

at my beginning: prairie

at my beginning: a town called   Normal

       on the far horizon   cornfield upon cornfield splayed

                flattened by tornado

        stunted stalks, palest soil under   a heavy sun

        soybeans   submerged in water

but no –   not far:

          today, tomorrow

KATHLEEN JAMIE

Kathleen Jamie was born in the west of Scotland in 1962. Her poetry collections to date include *The Overhaul* (2012 Costa Poetry Prize), *The Tree House* (Forward Prize) and *The Bonniest Companie* (2015 Saltire Scottish Book of the Year Award.) Her non-fiction includes the highly regarded essay collections *Findings* and *Sightlines*, which explore the confluence of travel, nature and culture. A new non-fiction book, *Surfacing*, will appear in 2019. Kathleen Jamie lives in Fife.

SELECTED POEMS

PICADOR | £14.99 | PBS PRICE £11.25

How good it is to have a *Selected* from Kathleen Jamie – to traverse, at one's convenience, the full range of her calm, hewn, disconcerting work in verse. She's an essayist, too: a travel-writer and nature-writer. Connections suggest themselves. Between, for instance, these short poems from her debut *Black Spiders* and from *The Tree House*:

No one knows if he opened his eyes,
acknowledged the dark,
felt around, found and drank
the mead provided, supposing himself
dead.
– 'Inhumation'

What kind of figure did he cut
huddled in the dusk, gut wound
packed with sphagnum,
as he sank into the bog
his offering of weaponry,
blades courteously broken,
his killed cherished swords?
–'Hoard'

SELECTOR'S COMMENT

Jamie blends matter-of-factness and surprise, observing acutely: she's intrigued by form, but also by the throb of life which eludes rigid structures. Writing at times in Scots, she may seem a poet of place, but one attuned to crossings between cultures: 'Karakoram Highway' is the road between Pakistan and China and 'The Queen of Sheba' turns an idiom – Who do you think you are, the Queen of Sheba? – into a springboard: "Scotland, you have invoked her name / just once too often / in your Presbyterian living rooms. / She's heard, yea / even unto heathenish Arabia / your vixen's bark of poverty." "Presbyterian", "vixen": I wonder at the hint, here, of Adrienne Rich's masterpiece 'Abnegation'.

Jamie, too, writes vigorously of women's lives. The aforementioned Queen of Sheba, for one: "the cool black skin / of the Bible couldn't hold her" (a mischievous line-break). 'The Green Woman' – "there's a word for women like us" (who've just given birth) – considers, with qualms, our plaudits for those who, passing the test, appear to have fulfilled their biological destiny. Mothers, that is, who've "risen, / tied to a ducking-stool, / gasping, weed-smeared, proven".

VIDYAN RAVINTHIRAN

KATHLEEN JAMIE

For forty years, I've been writing poems. Not every day, not even every year. But my relationship with poetry is the longest-standing I have, aside from that with my brother and sister.

Forty years, and I still can't offer a working definition of poetry. It seems to be my way of being in the world; the place where I am the best person I can be. And where I can encounter others, likewise, across space and time, also being their best.

One thing is for sure: it's not an exercise in "self-expression". It is absolutely not about "my voice". Making a poem is a work of noticing, clarifying, questing, negotiating and testing. And of course it's about listening, to the language and to a species of truth. Writing poems is where I discover what I think or feel, not where I go to express that.

This *Selected Poems* contains work from several collections, the first published when I was twenty, tapped out in an Edinburgh attic on an Olivetti typewriter. The most recent was published when I was fifty-three. Much has changed in that time, doubtless for the better, but I'm glad I'm not starting out now, lured before I'm ready by the Siren calls of social media, or feeling I ought to "perform".

A *Selected Poems* marks a change. Youth is certainly passed – so what comes next? It's difficult, in this moment, to celebrate, which is one of the poet's tasks. Another is to speak for, and speak to. To seek the "thou" in the world and to advocate for the voiceless non-human, whose fates we both hold and share. But I have learned something from these forty years of poetic practice: what's next probably won't be like what's gone before.

KATHLEEN RECOMMENDS

Last week in an Oxfam shop I picked up for £3 a copy of George Mackay Brown's *The Wreck of the Archangel* (John Murray), and was astonished by him, yet again. How could he sit alone in a wee council flat, wary of the world, and yet range so free! Here is lyric imagination and transformation, bardic confidence, child-like delight. We can easily get stuck in ourselves, even as poets, and be what we or others think we ought to be. We mustn't forget our imaginative possibilities.

RECOMMENDATION

We were always the first to get snow

SKEINS O GEESE

Skeins o geese write a word
across the sky. A word
struck lik a gong
afore I wis born.
The sky moves like cattle, lowin.

I'm as empty as stane, as fields
ploo'd but not sown, naked
an blin as a stane. Blin
tae the word, blin
tae a' soon but geese ca'ing.

Wire twists lik archaic script
roon a gate. The barbs
sign tae the wind as though
it was deef. The word whustles
ower high for ma senses. Awa.

No lik the past which lies
strewn aroun. Nor sudden death.
No like a lover we'll ken
an connect wi forever.
The hem of its goin drags across the sky.

Whit dae birds write on the dusk?
A word niver spoken or read.
The skeins turn hame,
on the wind's dumb moan, a soun,
maybe human, bereft.

Image: Gregory Hesse-Wagner

CHRIS McCABE

Chris McCabe has published five poetry collections, the most recent of which are *Speculatrix* and *The Triumph of Cancer*, both published by Penned in the Margins. He was shortlisted for The Ted Hughes Award in 2013 and his collaborative book with Sophie Herxheimer, *The Practical Visionary*, a collaged response to William Blake, has just been published by Hercules Editions. His creative non-fiction books include *In the Catacombs* and *Cenotaph South,* both Penned in the Margins, and his first novel, *Dedalus*, a sequel to *Ulysses*, is out with Henningham Family Press and has been described by *Literary Review* as "a complex and original work of fiction."

RECOMMENDATION

THE TRIUMPH OF CANCER

PENNED IN THE MARGINS | £9.99 | PBS PRICE £7.50

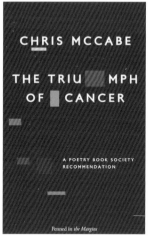

Chris McCabe's fifth book of poems, *The Triumph of Cancer*, begins with an epigraph from Gerard Manley Hopkins' journal of 1871: "For out of much more, out of little not much, out of nothing nothing: in these sprays at all events there is a new world of inscape." Along with instress, inscape can be broadly thought of as the stamp of a divinely conceived design on the living, whose individuality moves through the world with godly distinctiveness. Hopkins' notably enthusiastic poetic syntax, aimed at an inner sublime, is likewise often at play here in McCabe's fluxive and euphoric lines.

But beyond this, the usefulness of the design is brought into question by the physical and metaphorical order/chaos of cancer. Told to us in various ways, most poignantly through a son grappling with his father's impending death, cancer's narrative becomes a way of thinking through other disruptions at the level of all relations between self, other, meaning and loss. In 'Coupling', McCabe brings the linguistic and intimate into just such a dialogue with startling efficiency.

> These accidents of body & place called marriage.
> Or is it the destiny of genes that splits the union
> of two rings by one box into startled vernacular?
> My father a *victim*, my mother a *survivor*.

Throughout the book, the narrative of the father's life is being retrieved from the triumph of his cancer, as well as the underlying wishful son who engages him on his own terms, willing him, movingly, into time and place.

Elsewhere the reader is treated to McCabe's Joycean feats of humour. We discover a sharply literary sarcasm in his mock-Hopkinsesque poem 'Pinthover':

> ...O my director, emphatic Erdinger,
> take wing your banknote to browngold sustenance!

Albeit drawn into a constellation of friends, influences and poetic conspirators from Jackson Mac Low to John Donne, Bob Cobbing to Tom Jenks, Ted Hughes to Roddy Lumsden, there is a shifting, playful and dynamic confidence here that confirms McCabe is a truly singular voice.

SANDEEP PARMAR

| SELECTOR'S COMMENT

CHRIS McCABE

The Triumph of Cancer begins with a quote from Louis-Ferdinand Céline: "This body of ours, this disguise put on by common jumping molecules, is in constant revolt against the abominable farce of having to endure. Our molecules, the dears, want to get lost in the universe as fast as they can!" Celine's view, tone and authority over the inevitability of death set the perfect atmosphere for the concerns of my fifth collection. Why is that we watch a rose canker ("O rose thou art sick" as Blake wrote), and accept that as a part of nature, but it proves intolerable to us to watch a human, especially one we love, die of cancer? Isn't the arrangement that we're planted here for a number of seasons and then the inevitable happens?

Well try telling that to anyone watching the person they love die of cancer. I lost my father to the disease, a glioblastoma multiforme in the brain, when he was just fifty five. The word "Fight" was everywhere. Fight back! Beat cancer! But the "invisible worm" of the disease was stronger than any treatment available to him; the disease weakened him to the point of his family willing his killer, the cancer, to end his suffering. Since then my mother has had breast cancer and, through treatment and the life changes she made (and a mastectomy) is through the other side of it. We don't *fight* cancer, we use the human knowledge we have of it, and the treatments available, to give ourselves the best chance of survival. The language we're given to deal with cancer is skewed. In *The Triumph of Cancer* I wanted to untangle and re-thread that language, to make it complex in new ways.

Through these poems I explore cancer as a part of the inborn destructive paradox that is at the heart of all of nature. Still life poems and poems about objects mutate in and out of elegies and lyrics, as well as humorous poems about the disease. In the words of Siddhartha Mukherjee, whose book *The Emperor of All Maladies* was key to *The Triumph of Cancer*: "Cancer lives desperately, inventively, fiercely, territorially, cannily, and defensively – at times, as if teaching us how to survive."

CHRIS RECOMMENDS

James Brookes, *Spoils* (Offord Road); Kelvin Corcoran, *Facing West* (Shearsman) and *Article 50* (Longbarrow); Sarah Crewe, *floss* (Aquifer); Emily Critchley, *Ten Thousand Things* (Boiler House Press); Patricia Farrell, *High Cut: My Model of No Criteria* (Leafe Press); Yoshimasu Gozo, *Alice Iris Red Horse* (New Directions); Terrance Hayes, *American Sonnets for my Past and Future Assassin* (Penguin); Ishion Hutchinson, *House of Lords and Commons* (Faber); John Kinsella, *The Wound* (Arc); Alice Notley, *Certain Magical Acts* (Penguin); Antony Rowland, *M* (Arc); David Wheatley, *The President of Planet Earth* (Carcanet).

CHRIS MCCABE

THE TRIU MPH OF CANCER

With each death a desire for body. For witness. For song.

A POETRY BOOK SOCIETY
RECOMMENDATION

Penned in *the Margins*

X-RAY

Pierre & Marie Curie met in 1894 through their fascination with magnetism. They married a year later. *Radium, be near to me.* Where so many patients have seen their death through radioactivity they saw each other. Like the writer that chokes on their pen the breakthrough fluid Marie held in her hands killed her [leukemia]. Their daughter, Irene, disappeared into the future.

One evening, decades before, Pierre had walked through rain along the Rue Dauphine & slipped under a horse-drawn cart, crushing his skull unto death. *Radium, be near to me.* His father & lab assistant both said the same thing : his mind was elsewhere, thinking of a cure for cancer.

ROY McFARLANE

Roy McFarlane was born in Birmingham of Jamaican parentage and lived in Wolverhampton and the surrounding Black Country. Formerly Birmingham's Poet Laureate, now he's the Birmingham & Midland Institute Poet in Residence. His previous publications include *Celebrate Wha?* (Smokestack Books, 2011) and *Beginning With Your Last Breath* (Nine Arches Press, 2016). His latest collection looks at institutional racism, deaths in custody and a life story set at the turn of the millennium. He's also completing his MA in Writing Poetry with The Poetry School and Newcastle University.

RECOMMENDATION

THE HEALING NEXT TIME

NINE ARCHES PRESS | £9.99 | PBS PRICE £7.50

The title of Roy McFarlane's *The Healing Next Time* intentionally echoes James Baldwin's *The Fire Next Time*, a book of essays that crucially explored American racism in the 1960s. As Baldwin's thinking points to historical wrongs and redemption in a post-Civil Rights era, McFarlane's poems engage with violence from global terror, class struggles and racial divides in the first decade of the twenty-first century.

The section, 'New Millennium Journal', takes major global events like 9/11 and the invasion of Iraq as a backdrop for two minor figures: "family man" and "Jim", a community activist. What is fascinating about this sequence is the interplay between the tumult of the personal and political at all levels of experience, which McFarlane weaves together with references to religion, pop culture, sports, climate change, and, of course, the advent of the 24-hour news cycle. If healing is to be done, the poet suggests that redemption and progress requires the difficult task of both the "victim" and "oppressor" acknowledging and expanding their respective (sometimes contradictory) perceptions.

> But there's a rage, found
> between the reports of victims of race hate and the dailings of institutions.

Elsewhere, a series of poems on police violence recounts the unlawful deaths of men and women from Blair Peach to Mark Duggan, with a nod to Claudia Rankine's own similar project in *Citizen*. The book ends by offering love and hope as a way out of suffering.

Here under heaven in this hour let us breathe hope into a new millennium, let us believe in the humanity of others, let us harbour all that is honorable and heavenly

Breathe   Heaven is here, this hour, right now; let not the haves rob the have-nots of their heavenly moment here on earth, sowing seeds of separation.

Here under heaven we are the sum total of earth, air and water, alive with the fire which ignites the living soul. However abled, we are heavenly bodies,

ROY McFARLANE

'A Gift of a Rose' by Fred D'Aguiar from *British Subjects* was my first encounter with poetry that mirrored my African-Caribbean British experience and the events of the times. D'Aguiar poetically witnessed what was going on and left a marker. He articulated the outsider's experience, the racial discrimination and violence. He spoke of the beauty of being black living in Britain with a heritage flowing back to the Caribbean.

Twenty five years later and the poet's witness is still needed. Claudia Rankine in *Citizen* asked the question: "Will you write about Duggan? The man wants to know. Why don't you?" Along with conversations with Louis MacNiece, Paul Muldoon, Jill McDonough and James Baldwin, *The Healing Next Time* began to take form.

I begin the journey by looking back at the beginning of the new millennium – specifically the landmark Stephen Lawrence Report that brought the British public face to face with the issue of racism – as well as scouring through the events of the last fifty years regarding deaths in custodies, using fragmented, broken sonnets, sonnets morphing into their own shapes on the page, sonnets just trying to survive to tell their stories.

This collection is not tied down only in form but there's a freedom to use any form, to experiment, to negotiate, to stretch the possibilities of words on the page, a syncopation of jazz, a wondering Rasta looking at all our communities, looking at how we can become fully human in light of our failings.

Rita Dove once said "allow Black characters their full humanity by not covering up their shameful omissions and occasional cowardice, the ambivalence or spiritual failings", because "We are all human beings and therefore we err, sometimes horrifically; that is why we have forgiveness."

ROY RECOMMENDS

Claudia Rankine, *Citizen* (Penguin); Louis MacNeice, *Collected Poems* (Faber and Faber); Paul Muldoon, *Selected Poems* 1968-2014 (Faber and Faber); Jill McDonough, *Habeas Corpus* (Salt); James Baldwin, *The Fire Next Time* (Penguin); Terrance Hayes, *American Sonnets for my Past and Future Assassin* (Penguin); Hannah Lowe, *Chan* (Bloodaxe); Raymond Antrobus, *To Sweeten Bitter* (Out-Spoken Press); Inua Ellams, *#Afterhours* (Nine Arches Press); Tyehimba Jess, *Olio* (Wave Books); Layli Long Soldier, *Whereas* (Graywolf Press); Jacqueline Saphra, *All My Mad Mothers* (Nine Arches Press).

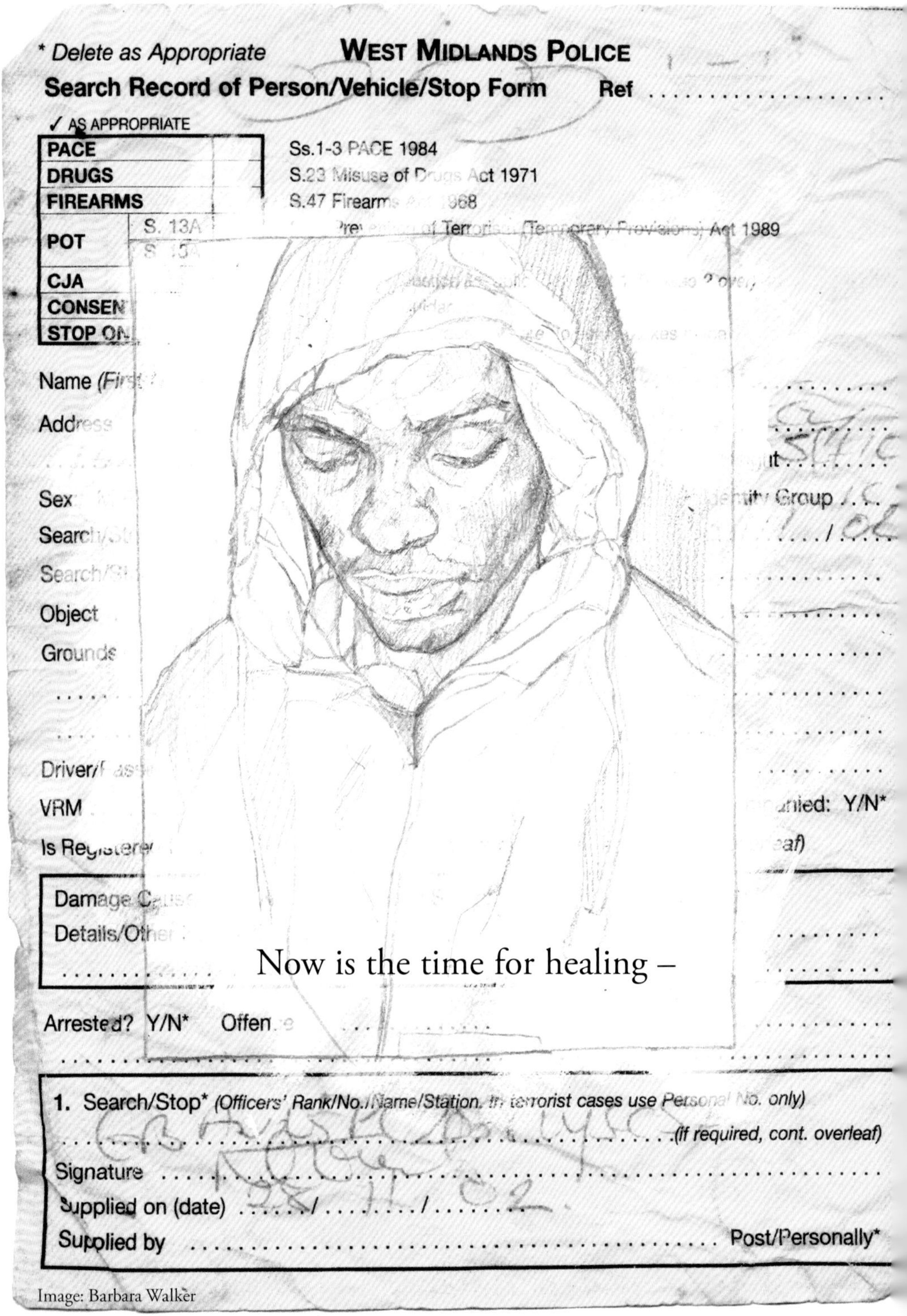

Now is the time for healing –

Image: Barbara Walker

RASHAN CHARLES, 2017

A man walks into a shop followed by a police officer, moments later he dies
A man walks into a shop, he's been walking along the well-worn paths,

over-lit with suspicions, and *you'll never amount to anything better,*
he's followed by an officer, he's thrown to the ground, struggles. He dies.

A man walks into a shop, he's followed, he's thrown to the ground, reflex or fear
he swallows something, his mouth is forced open, does it fucking matter. He dies.

A man walks into a shop wearing a cloak of survival in a world of drugs and violence,
where being black is an extra weight for young men on the streets of poverty. He dies.

A man walks into a shop I won't burden you with the weight of his twenty years
of living in a flak jacket of blackness, the need to be as swift as a basketball player
to step pass stop and search, glide past hard times. He dies.

A man walks into a shop, he's not white, headline news will make sure of that,
underline his unworthiness, label him before his body is laid down, libel him
before friends and family can speak good of him. It makes no difference. He dies.

A man walks out of a shop, notice he doesn't die. Outside a barbershop, he exchanges
the nod with elderly black men. He walks across the road to *Yo Rash what you saying?*
and he tells them it's all good. Elderly ladies laugh with him as he walks on by and
smile, *what a gentle, caring person.* He's still walking, a young girl hugs him because
he's the *guardian of the young.* Rash breaks bread with the beggars on the street, shares
the currency of time and now he rushes home to a daughter. Rash who dropped in
on the elders, *Mama P, I'm going to the shop, you want anything?* Notice he doesn't die.

JOHN AGARD

John Agard was born in Guyana and came to Britain in 1977. His many books include eight collections from Bloodaxe: *From the Devil's Pulpit* (1997), *Weblines* (2000), *We Brits* (2006), *Alternative Anthem: Selected Poems* (2009), *Clever Backbone* (2009), *Travel Light Travel Dark* (2013), *Playing the Ghost of Maimonides* (2016) and *The Coming of the Little Green Man* (2018). He was awarded the Queen's Gold Medal for Poetry 2012.

THE COMING OF THE LITTLE GREEN MAN

BLOODAXE | £9.95 | PBS PRICE £7.47

John Agard's little green man – the hero of these poem-tales – wanders our world in a state of good-humoured perplexity. Allergic to power and elusive of borders, he rejects (simply by being who he is) umpteen false moralities and has no time for either domination or denomination (he hates form-filling, for he doesn't know which identity-box to tick). Following only "the true north of his nose / losing himself to find himself", he can't claim to be an intellectual, but he's gifted with street-knowledge: a lovable flâneur, he is (with sceptical warmth) at home everywhere. While observing the excesses of our culture, he also counts his blessings:

The little green man
hasn't heard of Caliban

but he knows London
to be full of noises

that colonise the ear
with a thousand twanglings

of roadworks in progress
and scrapings of skyline.

Agard gives rollicking performances, and his verse is both easy to read and immediately ear-pleasuring – he is, however, as these Shakespearean lines suggest, an allusive poet alive to the lingering complexities of Empire. His little green man is a figure for the forced and unforced migrations of our times: he is a refugee, a tourist, both everyman and one-off freak. In fact he is unique – "In a world of the plural / being green keeps one singular". Eco-conscious ("I have many trees for allies / and so feel multiplied") he turns up on Question Time only for his question not to be answered, and acknowledges in himself the border-crossing, nationalism-undoing reality of genetic drift, which means that none of us are racially pure. Peering into our DNA, we realise that it's impossible ever to only come from, to only belong to, just one place:

Ah well, he's a long way from home
but wherever he lays his atoms
that's his genome.

SELECTOR'S COMMENT | VIDYAN RAVINTHIRAN

GETTING IT POLITICALLY CORRECT

Are those black
or non-white clouds
gathered in a huddle?

Is that white
or non-black snow
waiting to be shovelled?

The little green man
keeps such questions
to himself

preferring to jump
the fences of language
on ladders of love

not wanting to choose
between the non-white raven
and the non-black dove.

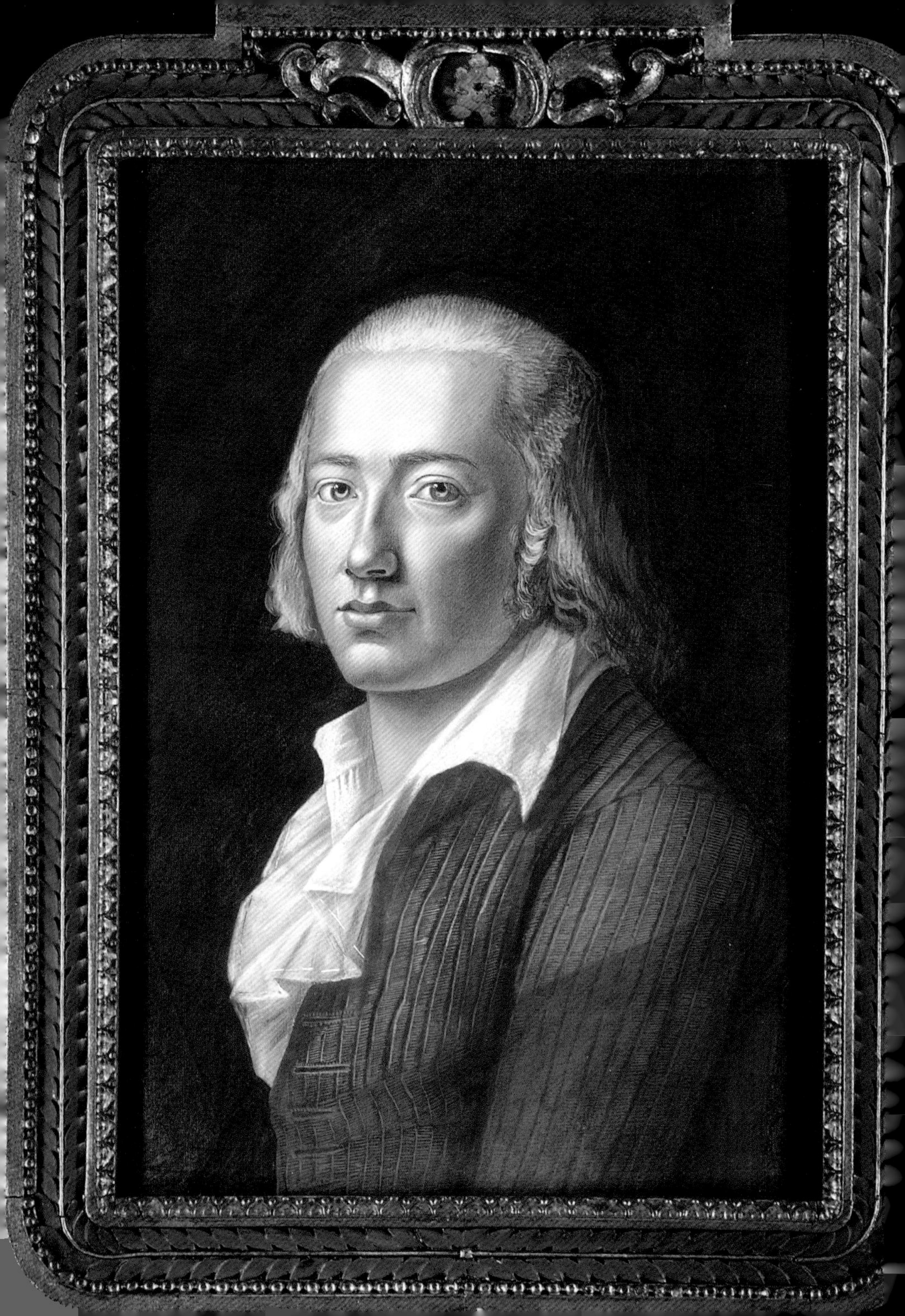

FRIEDRICH HÖLDERLIN

Friedrich Hölderlin was one of Europe's greatest poets (1770-1843). A major German lyric poet, his work bridges the Classical and Romantic schools. As a seminary student at Tübinger Stift, he studied Lutheran theology alongside the future philosopher Georg Wilhelm Friedrich Hegel. With his seminary classmate Isaac von Sinclair, Hölderlin was arrested for treason in 1805, but he was declared mentally unfit and institutionalised in 1806. He was released in 1807 and spent the rest of his life in the care of a foster family in a tower in Tübingen by the river Neckar.

David Constantine was born in 1944 in Salford. He read Modern Languages at Wadham College, Oxford, and lectured in German at Durham and Oxford. He has published ten books of poetry, five translations and a novel with Bloodaxe, as well as five collections of short stories with Comma Press. He received the Frank O'Connor International Short Story Award for *Tea at the Midland* and *In Another Country* was adapted into a major film starring Tom Courtney and Charlotte Rampling. He is a freelance writer, translator, a Fellow of the Queen's College, Oxford, and was co-editor of *Modern Poetry in Translation* from 2004 to 2013.

RECOMMENDED TRANSLATION

FRIEDRICH HÖLDERLIN

TRANSLATED BY DAVID CONSTANTINE

BLOODAXE | £14.99 | PBS PRICE £11.25

The choice this season has been particularly hard since there were a number of translations of major historical works as well as of contemporary poets new to me, books such as *Vagabond Sun*, Rimas Uzgiris' translations of the Lithuanian of Judita Vaičiūnaitė, Maura Dooley's *Negative of a Group Photograph*, her translations of the Iranian poet, Azita Ghahreman, and *An English Anthology* by the Belgian poet, Leonard Nolens, translated by Paul Vincent. All three are marvellously worth reading.

Among the major works on the other hand there is Jenny Lewis' bright and inventive version of *Gilgamesh Retold*, a selection of Rilke's *Notebooks and Personal Papers*, translated by David Need, and *Mea Roma*, new translations of Martial's epigrams by Art Beck.

If, after a lot of thought I have gone for David Constantine's much extended version of the German Romantic poet Friedrich Hölderlin's *Selected Poetry*, including over sixty new translations plus *Oedipus* and *Antigone* (translations of Hölderlin's translations) it is because Hölderlin is one of those vast figures who is, I suspect, rarely read and because Constantine is the leading poet-scholar associated with his work. In other words it is something of a landmark, probably the landmark Hölderlin for at least a couple of generations. The full and clear introduction by Constantine gives you the life and the career. As he tells us: "Hölderlin is the poet of absence... There is no poet more honest and uncompromising in the depiction of absence and loss." He is, in other words, a poet for our own lost times.

> Are the cranes coming home to you? Are the ships
> Resuming their course to your shores? Do breaths of the breezes
> We longed for move on your quietened waves? Does the dolphin,
> Lured from the depths, sun his back in the daylight again?

from 'The Archipelago'

HALF OF LIFE

The land with yellow pears
And full of wild roses
Hangs into the lake
O gracious swans
And drunk with kisses
You plunge your heads
Into the holy, the sober water.

Alas, for where in winter
Shall I come by flowers and where
The sunlight and
The shade of the earth?
The walls stand
Speechless and cold, the wind
Clatters the weathervane.

LIZ BERRY

Liz Berry is the author of *Black Country*, which won a Somerset Maugham Award, the Geoffrey Faber Memorial Prize and the Forward Prize for Best First Collection. 'The Republic of Motherhood' won the Forward Prize for Best Single Poem 2018. She lives in Birmingham, with her partner and their two sons.

THE REPUBLIC OF MOTHERHOOD

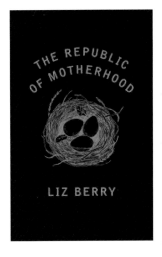

CHATTO   POETRY | £5

Opening with the line "I crossed the border into the Republic of Motherhood", Berry makes you a fellow traveller as she journeys into a new territory. A land with new expectations and new rules... and no guide book.

And that's where this beautifully assembled collection of poems steps in. Its dark blue cover with gold lettering makes it seem like a passport, or maybe a secular prayer book, a collection of hymns. Raising a child is one of the hardest things in the world and all those who embark on the journey are just expected to know what they're doing and get on with it. To admit that you're struggling is seen as weakness, so few would ever admit that "We are lonely / though never alone."

There's a wildness to the honesty about the realities of new motherhood. The poems feel so bold because they really connect. And none more so than Marie: "Marie, with your black hair / you could see I was drowning and taking him with me."

Alongside the tender, heart-breaking moments, there's humour and a visceral energy. These poems transport you, there's something primal in their intimacy you feel when reading them. Each poem is a re-creation, something that you experience as you read. For example, 'Sky Birth' leads you to the moment of birth:

> For a second we were alone on that highest place
> and love, oh love,
> I would have gladly left my body
> on that lit ledge for the birds to pick clean

Berry doesn't hold anything back with this collection, its beauty lies in her willingness to embrace the unspoken, the hidden. *The Republic of Motherhood* serves as that missing guide book – the wisdom and insight within its pages to be passed around amongst those finding their way into their new identity.

DEGNA STONE

The Pamphlet Choice is selected by Degna Stone and A.B. Jackson who draw up individual shortlists before making a joint decision. Degna Stone was mentored by Liz Berry as part of The Complete Works III.

THE STEPS

And this is where it begins, love –
you and I, alone one last time in the slatey night,
the smell of you like autumn, soil and bonfire,
that November the fourth feeling inside us.
There can be no truer wedding than this:
your bare hand in mine, my body winded
with pain, as you lead me to the car, to the
soon life. And we are frightened, so frightened –

Who will we be when we come back?
Will we remember ourselves?
Will we still touch each other's faces
in the darkness, the white noise of night
spilling over us, and believe there is nothing
we could not know or love?

Image: Christa Holka

SOPHIE ROBINSON

Sophie Robinson teaches Creative Writing at the University of East Anglia and is the author of *A* and *The Institute of Our Love in Disrepair*. Recent work has appeared in *n+1*, *The White Review*, *Poetry Review*, *The Brooklyn Rail*, *Ploughshares* and *BOMB Magazine*.

RABBIT

BOILER HOUSE PRESS | £11.99 | PBS PRICE £8.99

"At dusk each day i like to think / of all my new friends in different parts / of the city jerking off" is what we're told in the opening of the poem 'Art in America', the final piece in the 38-poem run that forms *Rabbit*. Defiantly arresting, Sophie Robinson's collection speaks to the fallout and turmoil of sexual abuse, hope, depression, lust, isolation and uncertainty. The poems present themselves in distorted modulations which crash into each other, rather than pretending to be in genial dialogue. And yes, there's a harshness, a rudeness even, which is wonderfully ameliorated by the wider themes the book takes on.

As the title implies there's a nefarious thing gnawing and pestering the root of Robinson's writing – a corrosive unease. A series of bitter misfortunes, a lasciviousness or an unsolicited waywardness. With little to no use of punctuation, ruptured forms, digital shorthand and no capitalisation, such decisions work to provoke the syntax into leaping from whatever startled it; to show how themes introduced at the start are later implicated into the book's grand narrative.

Robinson demonstrates poetic language's ability to fight for its individuality by fragmenting systems of logic through block text, or non-sequitur phrasemaking. This is what the collection does best, suspending its odd codes over such an expanse. In 'I Hate Flowers' the speaker declares: "all i want is sinking ships / all i want is ships under water / trains under water." Here we're directed towards a brutal intensity contrasted with the authority of fantasy, to make a thing drown, to destroy or submerge the impossible.

In 'Biggest Loser', the speaker episodically hands the reader a harrowing testimony, recounting several sexual assaults: "i'm twenty-nine now & since i was five / i have been sexually assaulted many times." It's a cruel and distressing piece which like much of the book employs a modern colloquium peppered with text-like Whatsapp abbreviations. These techniques serve to personalise the poems, reeling us towards those indiscretions with a candid prudence.

Rabbit is a meticulous spotlight. A cursory read might beguile the reader into perceiving the poems as some kind of "millennial shame", but in fact they are rich and exposing in their statement and posture. While being complex, human and wholly fragile, the arc once complete radiates with satisfying restoration.

SOPHIE ROBINSON

The poems in this book travelled with me across six years of my life, a time in which I fell in love, made a home in London with a partner, became a full blown alcoholic and drug addict, had a horrific break up, got sober, moved to Norwich, became obsessed with a much older lover, moved to New York, relapsed on alcohol, had a horrific detox, moved back to Norwich, and got sober again. So in many ways the poems are just what was happening, and the mood of how it was happening. The poems are not chronological exactly, but they still map the terrain of that narrative, I think.

The formal shifts in the work reflect this narrative, moving from the flat togetherness of the prose paragraph to the tidy verse intensity of poems like 'sunshine belt machine' or 'cancer, leo rising', to the expansive lostness, grasping and possibility held within the messy form of 'art in america'.

Thematically, what runs through the work are the three overlapping drives of obsession, devotion and addiction. I love using repetition far too much, pushing similes too far, and drowning myself in hyperbole. I often use poetry as a place to put feelings my body finds it hard to contain. The poem becomes my pet, my baby, my lover. It's the only thing my most shameful excesses can "make", rather than destroy.

As well as being a place for impossible excesses of feeling, I also always want poems to reach out towards the world, towards the reader. I try to make little gestures of inclusion through directness and tenderness of address and through humour. I want a reader to feel loved and cared for by this book, against the odds, in a world that makes it hard to love ourselves.

SOPHIE RECOMMENDS

Kaveh Akbar, *Calling a Wolf a Wolf* (Penguin); Sophie Collins, *Who Is Mary Sue?* (Faber); Amy Key, *Isn't Forever* (Bloodaxe); CAConrad, *While Standing in Line for Death* (Wave); Chase Berggrun, *R E D* (Birds); Ana Božičević, *Joy of Missing Out* (Birds); Rebecca Tamás, *Savage* (clinic); Danez Smith, *Don't Call Us Dead* (Chatto); Jameson Fitzpatrick, *Mr. &* (Indolent Books); Nuar Alsadir, *Fourth Person Singular* (Pavilion); Kristín Ómarsdóttir, *Waitress in Fall*, translated by Vala Thorodds (Carcanet); *Fondue*, A.K. Blakemore (Offord Road); *Not Here: A queer anthology of loneliness; Over There: A queer anthology of joy* (Tender Books).

BOOK REVIEWS

THE CAT IN THE TREBLE CLEF: LOUIS DE BERNIÈRES

Though well known for his novels, de Bernières is an accomplished poet; *The Cat in the Treble Clef* is a poignant, personal and keenly emotional collection, focused upon family and tragedy, his children and his grandmother. Interspersed throughout this book are beautifully rendered episodes from a life lived across the world. A delightful, moving and ultimately thought-provoking work.

HARVILL SECKER | £12.99 (HB) | PBS PRICE £9.75

SINCERITY: CAROL ANN DUFFY

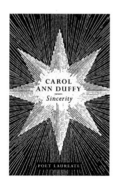

Carol Ann Duffy's final laureateship collection is the crowning glory of ten successful years as UK Poet Laureate. Ranging from moving tributes to recent events such as the Grenfell Tower fire to a comic commemoration of Trump's swearing in ceremony, this is the Poet Laureate at her most candid. Presented as a beautiful hardback and featuring a series of Christmas themed poems, this will be the perfect poetry stocking filler as well as a momentous volume to treasure for posterity.

PICADOR | £14.99 | PBS PRICE £11.25

GEN: JONATHAN EDWARDS

At the core of this collection is a musing upon the relationships between different generations. Starting from observations upon his own youth, Edwards reaches back into the lives of his parents and his grandparents from 2005 to '65 to 1905. He conjures an episode in the eighteenth-century life of Samuel Taylor Coleridge then fast forwards two hundred years to Richard Burton's dressing room. This is an intriguing collection, keenly focused upon the nature of people and their lives.

SEREN BOOKS | £9.99 | PBS PRICE £7.50

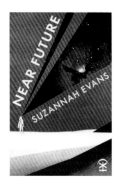

Evans' debut collection is preoccupied with the end of the world, the latent (or blatant) apocalyptic potential of the present. Evans deconstructs "the five kinds of apocalypse: nuclear, contagious, climatic, superintelligent, religious." Colossal fatbergs (the by-products of human excess) rub shoulders with robotic bees (created to keep the earth's dying ecosystem pollinated). This gloomy fare is rendered luminous by Evans' wit and poetic panache. An essential collection for survivalists, ecocritics and sci-fi enthusiasts.

NINE ARCHES PRESS | £9.99 | PBS PRICE £7.50

NEGATIVE OF A GROUP PHOTOGRAPH: AZITA GHAHREMAN
TRANSLATED BY MAURA DOOLEY & ELHUM SHAKERIFAR

A dual language selection spanning three decades of poetry by the Iranian poet Azita Ghahreman. The poet's own exile to Sweden, the suddenness of snow and her endless search for home pervade throughout. Haunted by memory and self estrangement, "that suitcase still holds a patch of the sky-blue me", poetry is a defence against the recurring "scarlet song" of war and words become our shared refuge: "She hides herself behind words / so that you have to search for her."

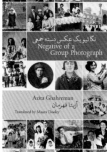

BLOODAXE | £12.00 | PBS PRICE £9.00

STOWAWAY: RICHARD GWYN

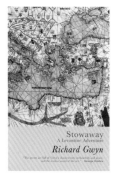

Cities and memories intermingle in the Levantine adventures of this seasoned traveller. Turkey, Venice and Beirut blur and "every city collapses into Byzantium". Gwyn conjures exotic escapism but urges us to question: "I could speak to you of / the spice markets of Antioch, / but don't you weary of all this second-hand exoticism?" These Calvino-esque tales take on a new poignancy in the age of migration, culminating with the poet's humbling visit to Lesbos at the height of the recent refugee crises.

SEREN BOOKS | £9.99 | PBS PRICE £7.50

BOOK REVIEWS

BOOK REVIEWS

GILGAMESH RETOLD: JENNY LEWIS

A vivid retelling of the epic of Gilgamesh, a world classic written in cuneiform on clay tablets discovered in the ruined library of the Assyrian King Ashurbanipal (c. 650 BC) under the Babylonian desert. These innovative tales are full of cosmic creation, dramatic battles, gods and grief. Lewis' evocative and exhilarating poems bring Gilgamesh to life for a whole new generation, discovering the resonance of ancient Mesopotamian myths in recent Middle Eastern conflicts and its enduring relevance today.

CARCANET | £12.99 | PBS PRICE £9.75

ANOMALY: JAMIE McKENDRICK

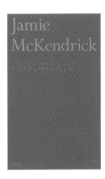

Urbane and primaeval, McKendrick's new collection plays with its own anomalies. This is arboreal poetry, "In the sacred wood / wrought poems hang", but entirely modern – an ode to a quince ends: "sent from my iphone". Full of nomadic echoes from Cervantes to Baudelaire, McKendrick moves from Italy to Liverpool, Bologna and Bombay. Always questioning, the collection ends with a poem about a bluffing newt, pretending to be alive or dead, we cannot tell.

FABER | £14.99 (HB) | PBS PRICE   £11.25

FROM NOTEBOOKS & PERSONAL PAPERS: RAINER MARIA RILKE
TRANSLATED BY DAVID NEED

Rainer Maria Rilke (1875–1926) is one of the greatest poets of 20th century European modernism. This bilingual volume presents the first ever English translation of these poems in the arrangement Rilke set down in 1926, a few months before his death. Paris poems sit alongside his 1906 Capri journal and is last poems. One of the most personal insights into Rilke yet which probes the limits of language and existence under "the great stars in the equinoctial night". A momentous addition to the Rilke canon.

SHEARSMAN | £14.95 | PBS PRICE £11.22

GREEN NOISE: JEAN SPRACKLAND

Sprackland has an incredible gift for description, her words leap off the page with great synesthetic prowess. The environment – the lived world of place, objects, memory and imagination – becomes so lucid and immediate as to be rendered strange and disorientating. From a depiction of aphid-farms managed by ants, to a meditation upon wild-swimming in a polluted river, a striking and varied assortment of subjects form a rich, disarming world of verse.

CAPE | £10.00 | PBS PRICE £7.50

THE AQI: DAVID TAIT

The smog and acid rain of Tait's home in China form a backdrop for this bold treatise upon political oppression. Contained within these pages are meditations upon censorship, state-sanctioned violence and hatred masked as freedom of expression. 'After Orlando', a breath-taking thirteen page epic, memorialises the Orlando gay nightclub shootings and decries the ways in which heteronormative societies allow prejudice to continue. Tait is a wordsmith, rallying his verse against an unjust and disturbing world.

SMITH | DOORSTOP | £9.95 | PBS PRICE £7.50

VAGABOND SUN: SELECTED POEMS: JUDITA VAIČIŪNAITĖ
TRANSLATED BY RIMAS UZGIRIS

The definitive selection of poems by one of Lithuania's greatest 20th century poets. Vaičiūnaitė captures the poetry of the city, winding streets, seagulls, markets, "cupolas, columns, bridges floating by". She digs deeper into the archaeology and architecture of Vilnius, giving voice to famous Lithuanian women from history to present *her*story. United by the feverish "vagabond sun", these poems are "full of lucid life" and a true celebration of "the noisy city of sun".

SHEARSMAN | £9.95 | PBS PRICE £7.47

BOOK REVIEWS

WINTER PAMPHLETS

MOON MILK: RACHEL BOWER

Bower presents a frank portrait of the journey from pregnancy to birth and motherhood with a deft poetic touch. This includes complex explorations of identity and how the body of the child and mother influence one another. Not only is *Moon Milk* a retort to the censorships and platitudes surrounding the experiences of motherhood, but it is a profound statement about the biology and psychology of creating (and maintaining) life – both good and bad, grotesque and beautiful.

VALLEY   PRESS | £7.99 |

FOR THE LOVE OF IT: DAVID CONSTANTINE

Layers of thought become slowly exposed in this finely crafted pamphlet which encourages thorough re-reading. Constantine's poems are haunted by various "will-o'-the-wisps". Death hides inside their stanzas, as does love and happiness. Constantine has a very individual way of examining the world, both tender and wry, but he also inhabits several different poetic voices. His view of humanity is generous, empathetic, and humorous. This is a quietly moving and deeply engaging pamphlet.

SMITH | DOORSTOP | £5 |

I WISH I HAD MORE MOTHERS: ANN GRAY

A tender and poignant pamphlet full of heartbreaking moments. These poems explore a mother's descent into dementia and quietly observe the surrounding seasons with a touching urgency. Domestic rituals from watching the washing machine to fending off a plague of ladybirds all reveal the quiet helplessness and strength of the poet-speaker. A truly moving account of aging, loss and love which will resonate with many.

SMITH | DOORSTOP | £5 |

TRUFFLE HOUND: LUKE KENNARD

Birmingham's Verve Poetry Festival launches an exciting experimental pamphlet series with long-awaited new poems from Luke Kennard. Kennard's distinctive sense of self-mocking humour shines throughout these immersive micro-narratives. Quirky, abitrary and at times inexplicable, these poems range from a song about 35p ibuprofen to a highly meta poem about cloning the poet himself. Kennard is the eternal truffle hound sniffing out society's foibles whilst wryly commenting on his own.

VERVE POETRY PRESS | £7.50 |

KNOWING THIS HAS CHANGED MY ENDING: ALEX MACDONALD

Knowing and not knowing intermingle enigmatically in this striking debut by an Eric Gregory award winner. The "real" world is only seen through a bus window and Modern Life is an unopenable bag of nuts. "Days become a series of rooms" and Macdonald seeks the videogame "noclip" cheat which allows us to walk through walls. His surreal wordplay – "not a clown in the sky" – probes the limits of language and the world as we know it, in which the ending, and knowledge, is constantly changing...

OFFORD ROAD BOOKS | £6 |

CHRISTMAS LIGHTS: TEN POEMS FOR DARK WINTER NIGHTS

Candlestick Press continues their tradition of Christmas pamphlets with this atmospheric and delicate anthology. Featuring poems by Kim Moore, Zaffar Kunial and Hannah Lowe, this sequence perfectly evokes the nostalgic – even primal – qualities of firelight burning against the winter dark, the quietness of winter cold, of home and hearth. There is nothing saccharine about these poems; this is a genuine, thoughtful and comforting anthology.

CANDLESTICK PRESS | £4.95 |

WINTER LISTINGS

NEW BOOKS

AUTHOR	TITLE	PUBLISHER	RRP
John Agard	The Coming of the Little Green Man	Bloodaxe	£9.95
Raymond Antrobus	The Perseverance	Penned in the Margins	£9.99
Peter Bennet	Mischief	Bloodaxe	£9.95
Ciaran Berry	Liner Notes	The Gallery Press	£10.50
Edmund Blunden	Selected Poems	Carcanet Press	£16.99
Martin Booth	The Knotting Poems	Shearsman Books	£9.95
Dennis Casling	New & Selected Poems	Smith|Doorstop	£9.95
Louis de Bernières	The Cat in the Treble Clef	Harvill Secker	£12.99
Julia Deakin	Sleepless	Valley Press	£10.99
Nick Drake	Out of Range	Bloodaxe	£9.95
Carol Ann Duffy	Sincerity	Picador	£14.99
Jonathan Edwards	Gen	Seren	£9.99
Carrie Etter	The Weather in Normal	Seren	£9.99
Suzannah Evans	Near Future	Nine Arches Press	£9.99
Ruth Fainlight	Somewhere Else Entirely	Bloodaxe	£9.95
Gabriel Fitzmaurice	Smitten Soul	Salmon Poetry	£10.00
Richard Gwyn	Stowaway	Seren	£7.99
Lee Harwood	HMS Little Fox	Shearsman Books	£9.95
Kathleen Jamie	Selected Poems	Pan Macmillan	£14.99
Maria Jastrzębska	The True Story of Cowboy Hat & Ingénue	Cinnamon Press	£8.99
John Kelly	Notions	Dedalus Press	£12.50
Paul Kingsnorth	Songs from the Blue River	Salmon Poetry	£10.00
Neetha Kunaratnam	Just Because	Smokestack Books	£7.99
Philip Larkin	Letters Home	Faber & Faber	£40.00
Guus Luijters	Song of Stars	Smokestack Books	£8.99
Char March	Full Stops in Winter Branches	Valley Press	£9.99
Chris McCabe	The Triumph of Cancer	Penned in the Margins	£9.99
Michael McCarthy	The Bright Room and other poems	Smith|Doorstop	£9.95
Karen McCarthy Woolf	Unwritten	Nine Arches Press	£14.99
Roy McFarlane	The Healing Next Time	Nine Arches Press	£9.99
Jamie McKendrick	Anomaly	Faber & Faber	£14.99
Rod Mengham	Grimspound & Inhabiting Art	Carcanet Press	£16.99
John Muckle	Mirrorball	Shearsman Books	£9.95
James Nash	A Bench for Billie Holiday: 70 Sonnets	Valley Press	£9.99
Doireann Ní Ghríofa	Lies	Dedalus Press	£12.50
Sophie Robinson	Rabbit	Boiler House Press	£11.99
Jane Routh	Listening to the Night	Smith|Doorstop	£9.95
Martin Rowson	Pastrami Faced Racist	Smokestack Books	£8.99
Sarah Shin & Rebecca Tamás, eds.	Spells	Ignota	£12.99
Ken Smith	Collected Poems	Bloodaxe	£14.99
Jean Sprackland	Green Noise	Jonathan Cape	£10.00
David Tait	The AQI	Smith|Doorstop	£9.95
Chérie Taylor-Battiste	Lioness	Valley Press	£9.99
Charles Tomlinson, ed. David Morley	Swimming Chenango Lake	Carcanet Press	£14.99
Jessica Traynor	The Quick	Dedalus Press	£10.00
Jean Watkins	Precarious Lives	Two Rivers Press	£9.99
John Welch	In Folly's Shade	Shearsman Books	£9.95
David Williams	Papaya Fantasia	Hedgehog Poetry Press	£9.99
Ross Wilson	Line Drawing	Smokestack Books	£7.99
Patricia Helen Wooldridge	Sea Poetics	Cinnamon Press	£8.99

TRANSLATIONS

AUTHOR	TITLE	PUBLISHER	RRP
Azita Ghahreman, trans. Maura Dooley & Elhum Shakerifar	Negative of a Group Photograph	Bloodaxe	£12.00
Friedrich Hölderlin, trans. David Constantine	Selected Poetry	Bloodaxe	£14.99
Jenny Lewis	Gilgamesh Retold	Carcanet Press	£12.99
Igor Klikovac, trans. John McAuliffe	Stockholm Syndrome	The Poetry Business	£5.00
Malathi Maithri, trans. Meena Kandasamy	Translating Feminisms: From South India	Tilted Axis Press	£6.00
Sulochana Manandhar Dhital, trans. Muna Gurung	Translating Feminisms: From Nepal	Tilted Axis Press	£6.00
Martial, trans. Art Beck	Mea Roma	Shearsman Books	£9.95
Leonard Nolens, trans. Paul Vincent	An English Anthology	Carcanet Press	£12.99
Rainer Maria Rilke, trans. David Need	From Notebooks and Personal Papers	Shearsman Books	£14.95
Nha Thuyen, trans. Kaitlin Rees	Translating Feminisms: From Vietnam	Tilted Axis Press	£6.00
Philip Terry	Dictator	Carcanet Press	£12.99
Doireann Ní Ghríofa	Lies	Dedalus Press	£12.50
F Starik, Maarten Inghels, trans. David Colmer	Lonely Funeral	Arc Publications	£11.99

PAMPHLETS

AUTHOR	TITLE	PUBLISHER	RRP
Andy Armitage	Letters To A First Love From The Future	Half Moon Books	£6.00
Graham Attenborough	New Face In Hell	Bare Fiction	£5.00
Charley Barnes	A Z-hearted Guide to Heartache	V. Press	£6.50
Charles Bennett	Thaw	Fair Acre Press	£5.99
Liz Berry	The Republic of Motherhood	Chatto & Windus	£5.00
Rachel Bower	Moon Milk	Valley Press	£7.99
Helen Charman	Support, support	Offord Road Books	£6.00
Sean Colletti	Saeculum	Bare Fiction	£5.00
David Constantine	For The Love of It	Smith|Doorstop	£5.00
Rebecca Cullen	Majid Sits in a Tree and Sings	Smith|Doorstop	£5.00
Charlotte Eichler	Their Lunar Language	Valley Press	£5.99
Ann Gray	I Wish I Had More Mothers	Smith|Doorstop	£5.00
Barbara Howerska	After the raging	Half Moon Books	£6.00
Luke Kennard	Truffle Hound	Verve Poetry Press	£7.50
Rachel Kerr	Sounding for home	Half Moon Books	£6.00
Sarah Law	My Converted Father	Broken Sleep Books	£5.00
Jane Lovell	METASTATIC	Against the Grain	£5.00
Alex MacDonald	Knowing This Has Changed My Ending	Offord Road Books	£6.00
Christopher North	The Topiary of Passchendaele	Smith|Doorstop	£5.00
Nigel Pantling	Hip Hind Hook	The Poetry Business	£5.00
Madeleine Wurzburger	Sleeve Catching Fire at Dawn	Smith|Doorstop	£5.00
Various	Ten Poems about Robins	Candlestick Press	£4.95
Various	Christmas Lights	Candlestick Press	£4.95

Poetry Book Society

THE STATIONERS' COMPANY

TIME
Productions

NO-ONE IS AN ISLAND

FRIDAY 23 NOVEMBER 2018 7.30PM

Sensual, god-fearing, terrifying, uplifting, joyous – poems and music that speak to our essential human connection in these fractious and turbulent times.

A collage of 17th-century and contemporary poems and music at St Martin within Ludgate, a beautiful and resonant Wren church.

Poems read by
Raymond Antrobus
•
David Harsent
•
& Reader at Large
Grace Cookey-Gam

Music performed by
Holly Cullen-Davies
&
Live Junction

Devised & directed by
Ian Grant

Produced by
Amy Liette Hunter

BOOK TICKETS:

Online: www.timeproductions.net
www.poetrybooks.co.uk
Tel.: The Poetry Book Society on 0191 230 8100

TICKETS: £20/£15 conc. (plus booking fee)

ST MARTIN WITHIN LUDGATE 40 Ludgate Hill, EC4M 7DC